WHY DO PEOPLE HARM ANIMALS?

© Aladdin Books 1988

Designed and produced by
Aladdin Books Ltd, 70 Old Compton Street, London W1V 5PA

Editor: Catherine Bradley
Design: Rob Hillier
Research: Cecilia Weston-Baker
Illustration: Ron Hayward Associates
Consultant: Angela Grunsell

Miles Barton is a producer at the BBC's natural history unit in Bristol.

Angela Grunsell is an advisory teacher specialising in development education and resources for the primary school age range.

Published in Great Britain in 1988 by
Franklin Watts Ltd, 12a Golden Square, London W1R 4BA

ISBN 0 86313 774 1

Printed in Belgium

"LET'S TALK ABOUT"

WHY DO PEOPLE HARM ANIMALS?

MILES BARTON

Gloucester Press
London · New York · Toronto · Sydney

"What is harming animals?"

People have killed animals for food, clothing and sport for thousands of years. But many people ask whether we should use animals in these ways. Are animals suffering unnecessarily at the hands of pet owners, zookeepers, farmers, scientists and hunters?

This book asks you to think about whether we have the right to harm animals by using them in the ways we do.

City farms enable city children to learn about farm animals.

Keeping a rabbit is nice for the pet owner. But is it all right for the animal to be kept indoors in a bedroom?

6

"Is it a good idea to keep pets?"

Many of us like to keep pets. Why do we like them? Perhaps it is because they depend on us, or because they give us affection. But what do we do for them?

Watching tropical fish or stroking a cat are pleasant things to do and they can help to calm us if we are upset. But is it all right to keep animals for our amusement? Yes, if we look after them well. But some pet owners do not. In cities many dogs are given too much food and not enough exercise.

The pet dog is often called "man's best friend". In the past dogs and humans looked after each other's lives. They protected people against enemies, such as animals and other humans. They also hunted down food for their owners. Now we have shops, we don't need dogs in the same way.

How kind are you to your pets? When you take on a pet, it needs a lot of care and attention. Hamsters and gerbils are easier to keep than most pets. But they need enough space. Many pets suffer in cramped cages or because of bad handling. Pets are not cuddly toys to be given as presents. They require regular feeding and care for many years.

Many people get a lot of pleasure from keeping a pet. Dogs need lots of exercise.

"Do people harm their pets?"

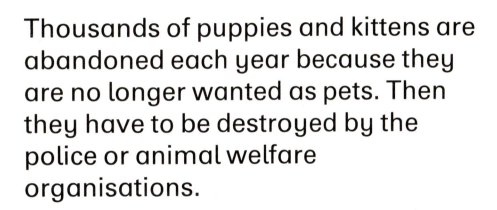

Thousands of puppies and kittens are abandoned each year because they are no longer wanted as pets. Then they have to be destroyed by the police or animal welfare organisations.

Sometimes a pet has to be left with other people. Always make sure the person looking after your pet will look after it properly.

Leaving a pet at a kennel when you go on holiday can be a bit worrying.

11

"Is it cruel to keep animals in a zoo?"

Getting close to wild animals in a zoo is fun. We can learn a lot from animals. Small animals, such as chipmunks, can have all the space they need and are ideal zoo animals. However, large animals such as elephants, polar bears or dolphins become bored in a zoo enclosure. Some of them need company and plenty of space, which they cannot always get in a zoo.

> Some people think if you can see wild animals on television, you don't need to see them in a zoo.

Many wild animals have already died out because of human activity and many more are threatened. They need wild places left alone so they can survive. We need to try to balance our needs with wild animals' needs.

Zoos can help to save animals in danger. Good zoos can teach people how ainimals live in their natural homes, and how important it is to preserve the places they live in. This can lead to animals being protected in the wild. Zoos can also help animals which have nearly become extinct. They can breed animals in zoos and then put them back in the wild.

European bison at Whipsnade zoo were saved from extinction by being bred in zoos.

The gorillas in Central Africa have been saved because people now protect the forests they live in.

"Do people harm wild animals?"

Some wild animals, like the rhino and the elephant, need special protection because they are killed for their tusks and horns. These are used as ornaments. All over the world wild birds and animals are harmed because the places they live in are being used by humans and they have nowhere to live.

We also produce wastes which pollute the rivers and the seas. This damages and kills fish and the sea mammals that feed on them.

17

"Should we wear animal furs as clothing?"

Some people like to wear animal fur because they think it looks beautiful. In the past people wore animal fur because it was the only material available to keep them warm. Today warm clothing can be made from plant products or man-made substances, like polyester or nylon. But animals are still killed to make fur coats. Foxes, beavers, minks and wild cats are caught and shot.

A bag made from the fur of a margay small cat. Wild cats are becoming rare and need protection.

A trader sells furs in China. For some people this is the only way they can make a living.

Cows provide us with milk and also beef.

"What about farm animals?"

People have eaten meat for thousands of years. Until recently animals were raised on small farms. Their owners knew the better they treated them the better the food.

Nowadays much meat is "factory farmed" – the largest number of animals are raised in the smallest possible space. This means everyone in cities can eat cheap meat, milk and eggs. Not everyone agrees that we should eat meat at all.

21

"What is the cost of cheap meat?"

On many modern farms chickens are kept in small wire cages which are too small. In some countries this type of farming is being made illegal. Small improvements in factory farming would improve millions of animals' lives. But the farmer and the food company would want the same profit. So the price of meat in the shops would go up.

Keeping chickens in wire cages means they lay more eggs than they would in the farmyard.

23

"Should we use animals to test drugs?"

Animals are used by scientists to investigate how bodies work and sometimes to find ways of curing diseases. If scientists did not do this, people would have to risk their lives and health to try out new drugs.

Some people say we shouldn't use animals to do things we wouldn't get humans to do. But do animals feel the same way as we do? Animals can feel pain but because they are not as intelligent as us, many people think they cannot suffer as much as we do.

24

Shampoo, soaps and lipsticks are also tested on animals. But is it worth hurting rabbits for a new shampoo? Some products do not use animals for testing.

"Should we use animals for entertainment?"

Animals have been used to entertain people for thousands of years. Some cruel sports, such as bear baiting or cock fighting, have been stopped. But animals are still hunted for fun. People pay to shoot lions in Africa.

Sometimes the numbers of one animal in an area become too large for its own survival and that of other species. Therefore hunters say that they are not harming animals by killing some. Many people think this is cruel.

26

Many countries do not allow circuses to use animals because they think it harms them.

"Do we need to harm animals?"

Our relationship with animals is changing. We need them less for protection and food gathering. But we want them more for other reasons, like testing drugs, comforting lonely people and providing millions of city dwellers with meat.

People harm animals when they put human needs before animal needs. Animals, plants and humans all live in the same world and depend on each other. We need to respect animals' needs for our own sake.

We still use sheep to provide wool and meat. Yet when they are farmed in large sheep stations they can suffer from neglect. Farm animals need looking after.

29

"What can I do?"

You may agree or disagree with some of the uses of animals in this book. However you will probably all agree that no one should harm their pets. You probably want to think a lot more about why people harm animals.

You could find out more about the way animals are treated on farms, in homes and in the wild. Make sure you look after your pets properly and give them the food, space and excercise they need.

You can feed wild birds and put up bat and bird boxes. You could create a pond in your garden for frogs and newts and encourage your friends to do the same.

Useful addresses

Royal Society for the Prevention of Cruelty to Animals
For advice on how to keep pets and for information about cruelty to animals.
RSPCA Headquarters, Causeway, Horsham, West Sussex RH12 1HG.

Royal Society for the Protection of Birds
For advice on feeding wild birds, bird-boxes etc.
The Lodge, Sandy, Bedfordshire SG12 2DL.

World Wide Fund for Nature
For information about wild animals in danger throughout the world.
Panda House, Weyside Park, Godalming, Surrey GU7 1XR

Fauna and Flora Preservation Society
For information on bat boxes and ponds etc as well as campaigns such as "Help a toad across the road".
8-12 Camden High Street, London NW1 0JH.

Young People's Trust for Endangered Species
For information about preservation of wild animals, plants and wilderness areas.
19 Quarry Street, Guildford, Surrey GU1 3EH.

Watch Club/Royal Society for Nature Conservation
For information about nature projects and conservation.
The Green, Nettleham, Lincoln LN2 2NR.

Index

Photographic Credits:
Cover: Robert Harding; pages 5, 9
and 14: Network; pages 6, 13, 22
and 29: Sally and Richard
Greenhill; pages 10, 19 and 23:
Spectrum; page 16: Survival
Anglia; pages 20, 25 and 27: Zefa.

PRINTED IN BELGIUM BY
proost
INTERNATIONAL BOOK PRODUCTION

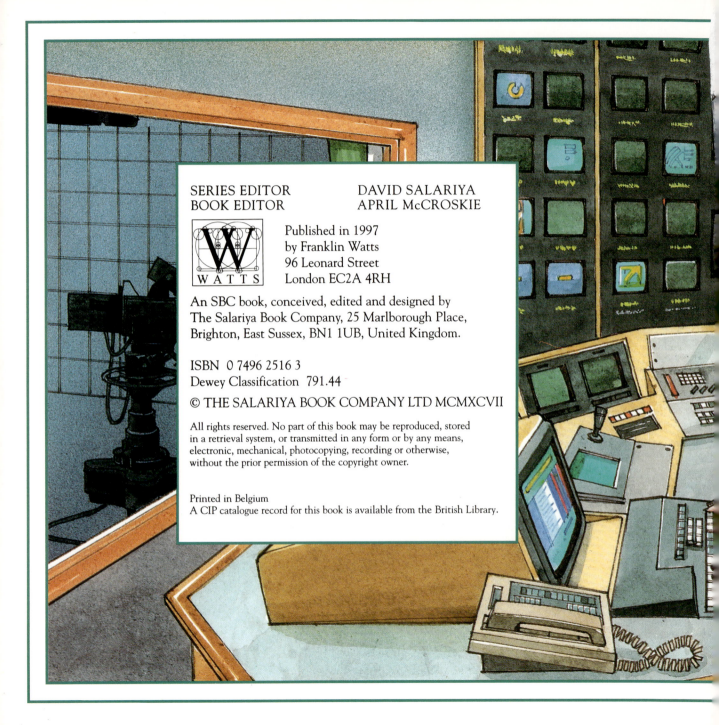

SERIES EDITOR   DAVID SALARIYA
BOOK EDITOR   APRIL McCROSKIE

Published in 1997
by Franklin Watts
96 Leonard Street
London EC2A 4RH

An SBC book, conceived, edited and designed by
The Salariya Book Company, 25 Marlborough Place,
Brighton, East Sussex, BN1 1UB, United Kingdom.

ISBN 0 7496 2516 3
Dewey Classification 791.44

© THE SALARIYA BOOK COMPANY LTD MCMXCVII

Printed in Belgium
A CIP catalogue record for this book is available from the British Library.

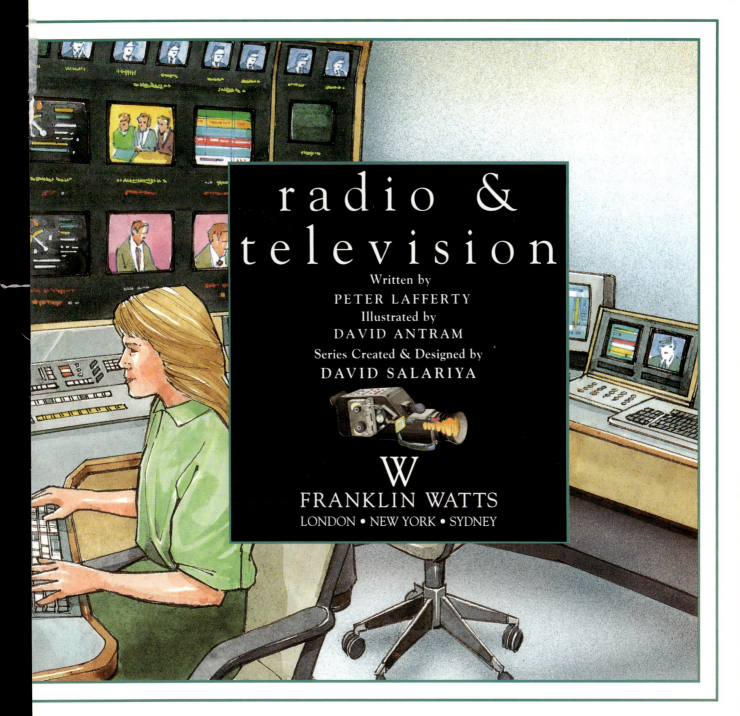

radio &
television

Written by
PETER LAFFERTY
Illustrated by
DAVID ANTRAM
Series Created & Designed by
DAVID SALARIYA

W
FRANKLIN WATTS
LONDON • NEW YORK • SYDNEY

CONTENTS

Television and radio

are an important part of modern life. We can listen to music and news on the radio and we can watch our favourite game shows and dramas on television.

Programmes are produced at a radio or television station. They are then carried by invisible waves, called electromagnetic waves, to our homes. These waves travel at great speed. A radio or television wave can go around the world seven times in a second. Radio and television sets catch the waves and turn them into pictures and sound.

Electromagnetic waves were

discovered in 1888 by German scientist, Heinrich Hertz. Guglielmo Marconi of Italy used these waves to send messages over a long distance. In 1901 he sent a message across the Atlantic Ocean from England to Canada. In 1925 Scottish inventor, John Logie Baird, discovered how to use electromagnetic waves to send pictures and built the first television set.

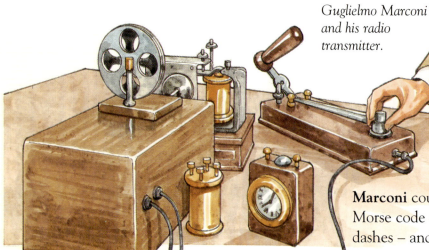

Guglielmo Marconi and his radio transmitter.

Marconi could only send messages in Morse code – a series of dots and dashes – and not as speech.

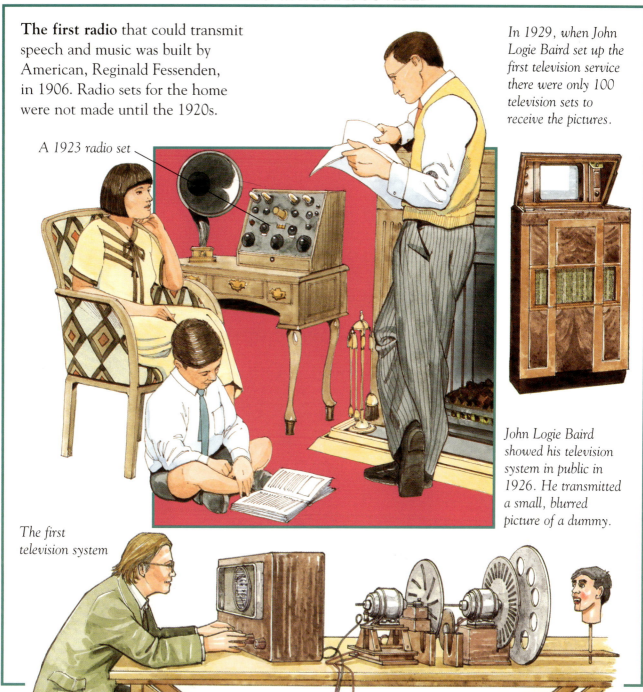

The first radio that could transmit speech and music was built by American, Reginald Fessenden, in 1906. Radio sets for the home were not made until the 1920s.

In 1929, when John Logie Baird set up the first television service there were only 100 television sets to receive the pictures.

A 1923 radio set

John Logie Baird showed his television system in public in 1926. He transmitted a small, blurred picture of a dummy.

The first television system

The transmitter sends the waves and the receiver catches them.

The distance between wave crests is called the wavelength.

Wave crest

If the rope is moved quickly, the waves have a short wavelength.

There are many electromagnetic waves, each with a different wavelength. Radio and television waves have long wavelengths.

When one end of a rope is moved up and down, waves travel along it. Electromagnetic waves are like the waves in a rope. But you cannot see electromagnetic waves and a rope is not needed to carry them. Electromagnetic waves are invisible ripples of electric and magnetic force which can travel through empty space. They travel at a speed of 300,000 kilometres per second.

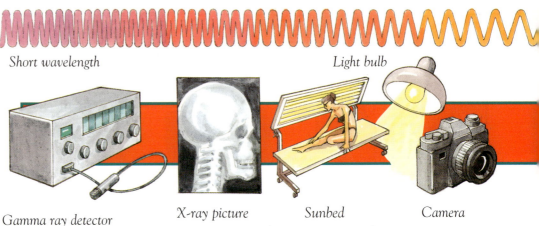

Gamma rays   X-rays   Ultraviolet rays   Visible light

Short wavelength

Light bulb

Gamma ray detector   X-ray picture   Sunbed   Camera

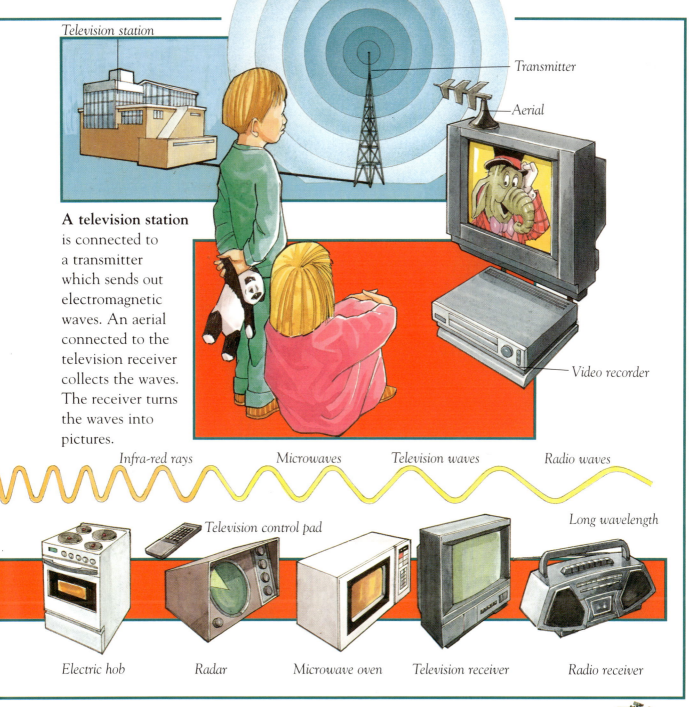

Television station

Transmitter

Aerial

A television station is connected to a transmitter which sends out electromagnetic waves. An aerial connected to the television receiver collects the waves. The receiver turns the waves into pictures.

Video recorder

Infra-red rays   Microwaves   Television waves   Radio waves

Long wavelength

Television control pad

Electric hob   Radar   Microwave oven   Television receiver   Radio receiver

11

Radio announcers

speak into a microphone. Microphones produce an electrical signal which varies as the spoken words vary. The microphone signal is sent to the transmitter. The transmitter produces a radio wave, called a carrier wave. The microphone signal is mixed with the carrier wave. This produces a radio wave which varies as the microphone signal varies. The radio wave is then broadcast from the aerial.

Metal plate

Wire coil

A metal plate moves when sound falls on a microphone. This produces an electrical signal in a wire coil attached to the plate.

The process of mixing the signal from the microphone with the carrier wave is called modulation.

Microphone

Transmitter

Aerial

Announcer

Tape player

As well as a microphone, a radio studio may have record and tape players. This equipment produces a signal which is mixed with the carrier wave for broadcasting.

Singers often use radio microphones. Inside the microphone is a small radio transmitter. The words of the song are sent to a receiver connected to a loudspeaker system and made louder.

Radio microphone

Radio and television aerials are mounted on a communications tower. Many countries have a network of towers.

A satellite dish beams television signals to a satellite in space 35,880 kilometres above the Earth.

A transmitter tower beams signals direct to our homes. The higher the tower, the further it can transmit signals.

People were amazed when Marconi sent a radio message across the Atlantic Ocean. How could radio signals travel such a long way? The answer is that some radio waves can bounce off a layer in space called the ionosphere. The ionosphere is like a mirror reflecting signals to distant places.

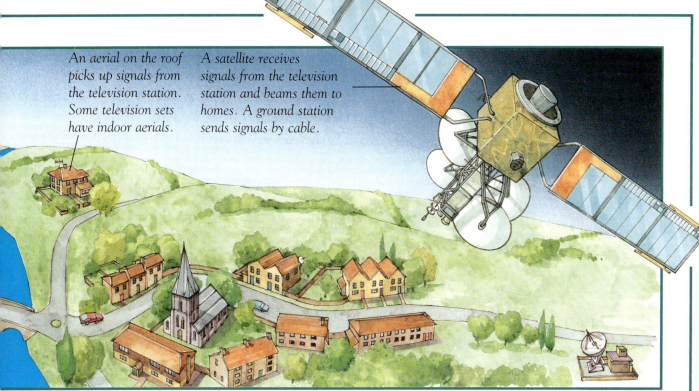

An aerial on the roof picks up signals from the television station. Some television sets have indoor aerials.

A satellite receives signals from the television station and beams them to homes. A ground station sends signals by cable.

Television signals pass through the ionosphere. So satellites are used to bounce these signals back to the ground.

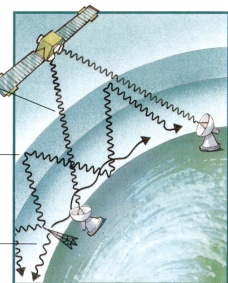

Very short-wave signals pass through the ionosphere and are picked up by satellites.

Short-wave radio signals bounce off the ionosphere and are reflected downwards.

Some radio waves travel without being reflected.

Most modern radios contain silicon chips. These small chips contain many parts connected together into complex circuits.

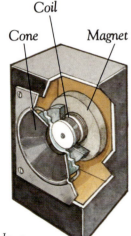

Cone Coil Magnet

In a loudspeaker, an electrical current flows through a wire coil near a magnet. The force produced moves the coil. A paper cone attached to the coil vibrates to make sound.

When radio waves pass over the aerial of a radio receiver, they cause electrical currents to flow in the aerial. The receiver changes these electrical currents or signals into sounds. The currents flow to the tuning circuit, which picks out the signals from the radio station. Then, the signal is amplified (made stronger). A decoder separates the audio (sound signal) from the carrier wave. The audio signal is amplified again until it is strong enough to work a loudspeaker. The loudspeaker makes the sounds we hear.

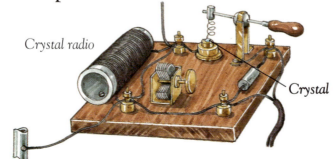

Crystal radio

Crystal

In a crystal radio set, a crystal acts as a decoder to separate the audio signal from the carrier wave.

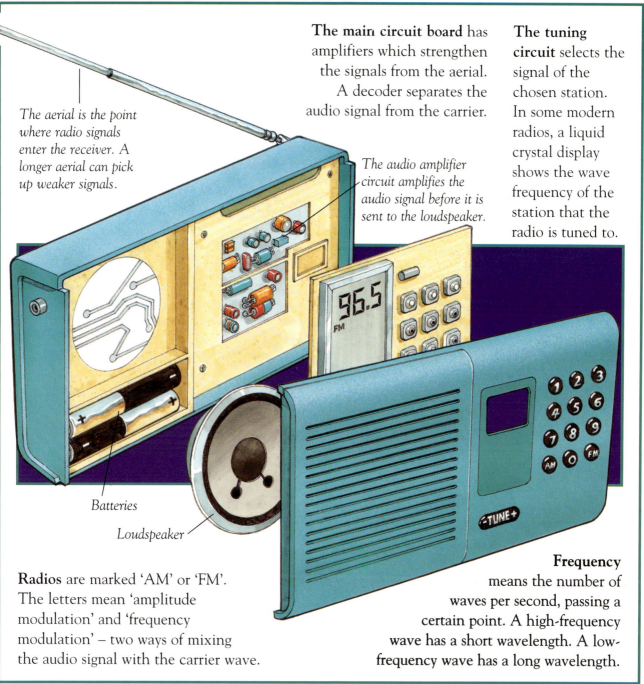

The aerial is the point where radio signals enter the receiver. A longer aerial can pick up weaker signals.

The main circuit board has amplifiers which strengthen the signals from the aerial. A decoder separates the audio signal from the carrier.

The tuning circuit selects the signal of the chosen station. In some modern radios, a liquid crystal display shows the wave frequency of the station that the radio is tuned to.

The audio amplifier circuit amplifies the audio signal before it is sent to the loudspeaker.

Batteries

Loudspeaker

Radios are marked 'AM' or 'FM'. The letters mean 'amplitude modulation' and 'frequency modulation' – two ways of mixing the audio signal with the carrier wave.

Frequency means the number of waves per second, passing a certain point. A high-frequency wave has a short wavelength. A low-frequency wave has a long wavelength.

Presenters sit in a soundproof room, called a studio, and speak into a microphone. The producer watches through a window and gives instructions.

Making a radio programme

involves many different people. The producer is in control and decides the order of items in the programme, plus their length and style. The presenter, or DJ (disc jockey), for music shows, is the person whose voice is heard by listeners. Engineers make sure that the programme goes to the transmitter and is broadcast correctly.

Most radio stations keep records and CDs in a music library. They are often supplied free by record companies.

The presenter sits at a control desk or mixer. This has faders – sliding knobs that control the volume of sound from the microphones, record turntables, CD players and tape players.

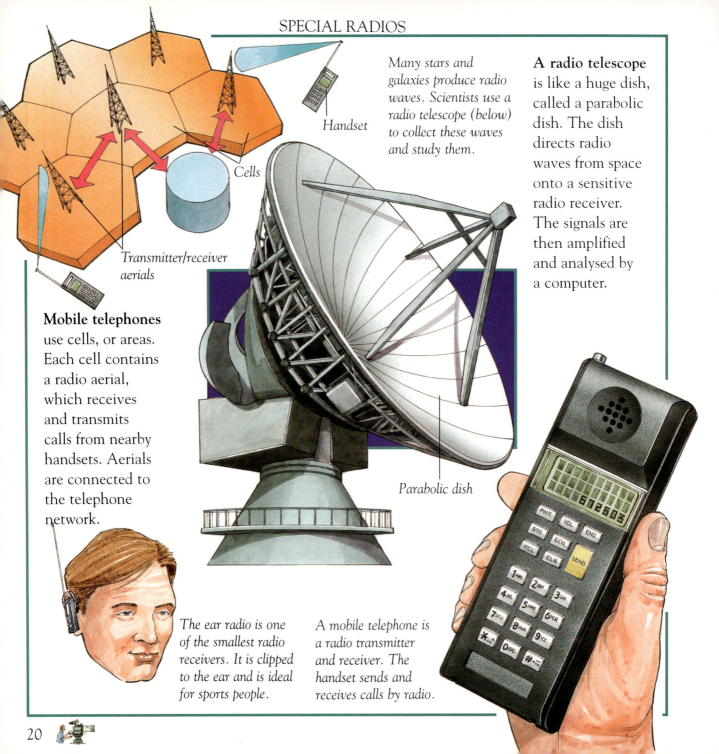

Handset

Cells

Transmitter/receiver aerials

Many stars and galaxies produce radio waves. Scientists use a radio telescope (below) to collect these waves and study them.

A radio telescope is like a huge dish, called a parabolic dish. The dish directs radio waves from space onto a sensitive radio receiver. The signals are then amplified and analysed by a computer.

Mobile telephones use cells, or areas. Each cell contains a radio aerial, which receives and transmits calls from nearby handsets. Aerials are connected to the telephone network.

Parabolic dish

The ear radio is one of the smallest radio receivers. It is clipped to the ear and is ideal for sports people.

A mobile telephone is a radio transmitter and receiver. The handset sends and receives calls by radio.

Radio is used for listening to programmes in our homes. But it is used for communication and for talking to other people also. At an airport, air traffic controllers use radio to talk to arriving and departing aircraft. The police use radio to keep in touch with patrols and cars on the streets. Truck drivers talk to other drivers using citizens' band or CB radio. CB radio can transmit over a short distance only.

Truck drivers using a CB radio can exchange information about the traffic and the weather conditions.

On a video tape, pictures and sound are recorded as magnetic patterns on plastic tape. The picture is recorded diagonally across the tape and sound is recorded along the edge of the tape.

— *Plastic tape*

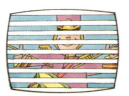

The electron beam scans (moves over the screen) twice to form the picture.

The first scan misses out every second line. The second scan fills in the missed lines.

The picture is formed from the two scans. Each second, 25-30 pictures are formed.

A television set has an aerial like a radio receiver. This picks up signals from a television station. Part of the signal carries the picture and part carries the sound. Inside the television, the sound signal is sent to the loudspeaker. The picture (or video) signal is sent to the television tube. The picture is formed on one end of the tube when a beam of electrical particles, called electrons, zigzags across the screen in horizontal lines.

In a colour television, three electron beams are produced by three guns at the narrow end of the tube. There is a gun for each colour – red, green and blue.

The electron beams scan across the screen at the large end of the tube. Where a beam strikes the screen, it produces a dot of light.

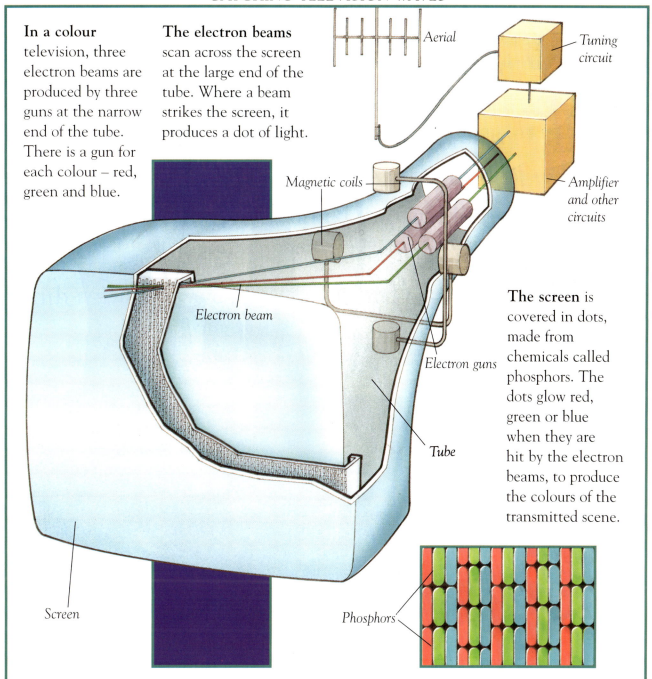

Aerial

Tuning circuit

Amplifier and other circuits

Magnetic coils

Electron beam

Electron guns

Tube

The screen is covered in dots, made from chemicals called phosphors. The dots glow red, green or blue when they are hit by the electron beams, to produce the colours of the transmitted scene.

Screen

Phosphors

Television studios are very busy places.

As well as the presenter, there are several cameras in the studio. The camera operators wear headphones to hear instructions from the director. Overhead, bright lights shine on the presenter and studio guests. The studio manager, also wearing headphones, rushes around making sure everything runs smoothly.

Monitor

The director sits in a separate control room. He or she decides which of the pictures shown by the cameras should be broadcast and gives instructions to the camera operators. Monitors show the picture shots from each camera.

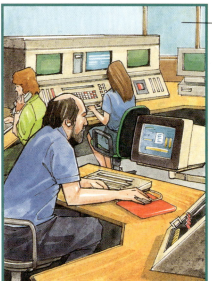

In the video control room, engineers check the quality of the picture before it is broadcast. They may operate the video tape recorders also.

Sound engineers are in a separate control room. They select the sounds from the microphones and add special effects or music.

The director produces a storyboard before a drama is filmed. It has sketches to show what shots are needed and what each shot should look like.

Storyboard

Camera operator

Assistant

Sound engineer

Microphone

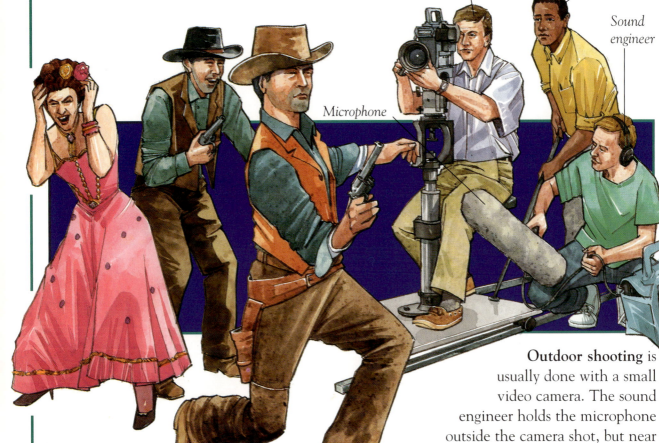

Outdoor shooting is usually done with a small video camera. The sound engineer holds the microphone outside the camera shot, but near enough to pick up the actors' voices.

Television

programmes need to be well-planned. For a game show, the questions have to be written. For an adventure or drama, the script has to be written to tell the actors what to say and do. Next come rehearsals, when each part of the programme is practised. If rehearsals go well, the programme is filmed.

Make-up is applied by a make-up artist. The make-up is touched up during filming.

Edit pair

After filming, the editor combines the film or video tape of the scenes in the correct order. The editor uses two electronic machines, called an edit pair, for this job.

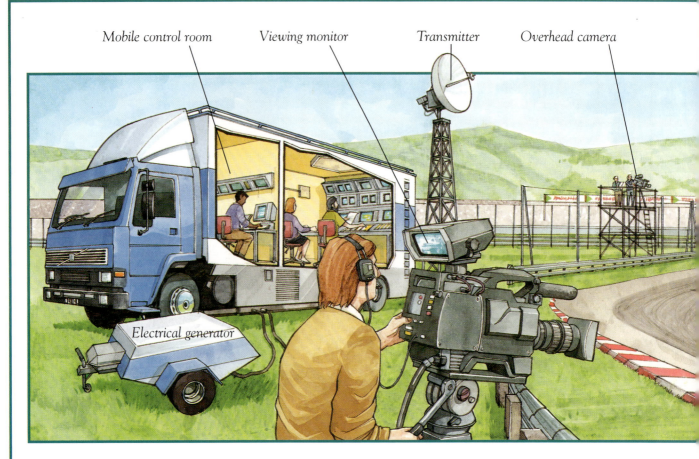

Mobile control room   Viewing monitor   Transmitter   Overhead camera

Electrical generator

Television programme makers must sometimes go to an event and broadcast the programme from there. This is called an outside broadcast. Sports events might be televised in this way. A specially equipped truck is used as a mobile control room.

Reporter

Microphone

Tape recorder

Pictures recorded by the cameras are watched by the director. Pictures may be recorded on tape or sent back to the studio using a transmitter connected to the control room.

Radio reporters often use portable tape recorders when they interview people. The tape is edited to remove background noises before broadcasting.

A television picture

can be altered to produce amazing special effects. The shape, colour and size of the picture can be altered. The picture can be stretched, squashed or flipped over. These special effects are made by machines that change the signal producing the picture. Other special effects are produced by combining the signals from different cameras.

Computers can copy part of a picture and reproduce it at different positions on the screen. Many advertisements are made using these techniques, called computer graphics.

Some televisions have a screen that can be split into sections, called windows. Each window can show a different programme. More than one programme can be watched at a time.

Window

Chroma-key is a technique used to produce weather forecasts. The presenter is filmed against a blue background. Another camera films the weather map. The pictures are mixed so the presenter appears to be in front of the map. This prevents shadows falling on the map.

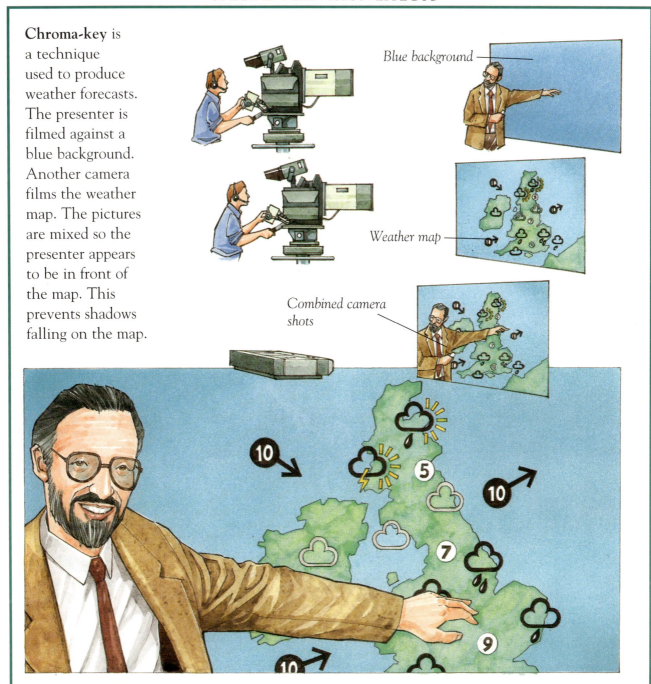

Blue background

Weather map

Combined camera shots

33

Camera

A helicopter
is used to film the
overhead view at
some sports
events. Pictures
are beamed back
to screens in the
stadium.

Televisions are not only
found at home. They are used in
many other places. Television
cameras record people in the street or in
banks and shops. If a robbery occurs, the film
or video record can help find the robbers.
Giant television screens are found at sports
events. They show the action, in close-up, as
it happens. Small television sets can even be
carried by hikers in the countryside.

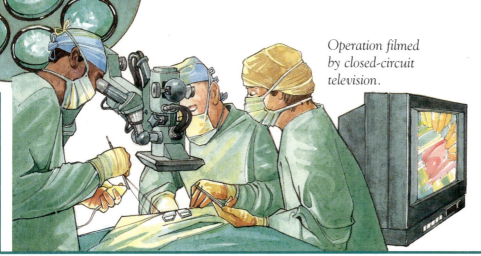

*Operation filmed
by closed-circuit
television.*

An operation
can be filmed and
watched on
monitors by
medical students
in nearby rooms.
This is called
closed-circuit
television.

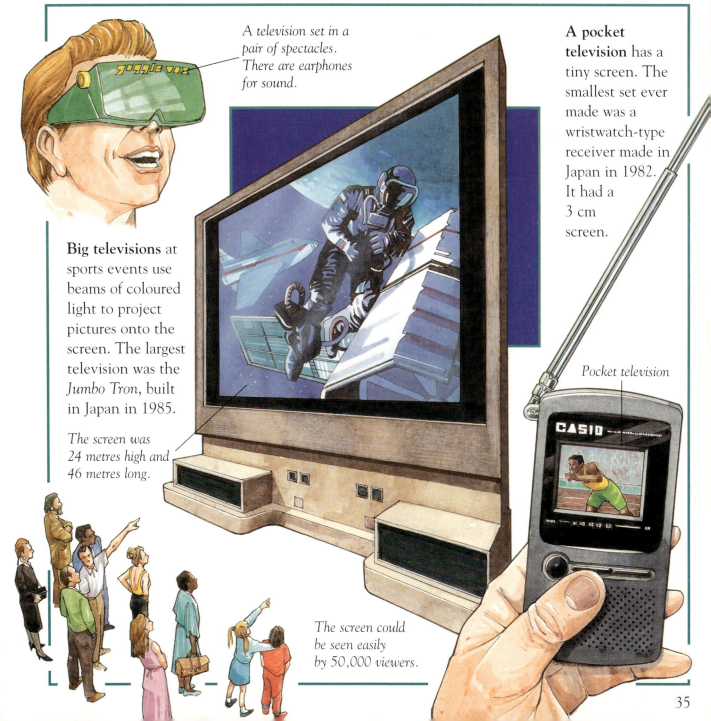

A television set in a pair of spectacles. There are earphones for sound.

A pocket television has a tiny screen. The smallest set ever made was a wristwatch-type receiver made in Japan in 1982. It had a 3 cm screen.

Big televisions at sports events use beams of coloured light to project pictures onto the screen. The largest television was the *Jumbo Tron*, built in Japan in 1985.

The screen was 24 metres high and 46 metres long.

Pocket television

The screen could be seen easily by 50,000 viewers.

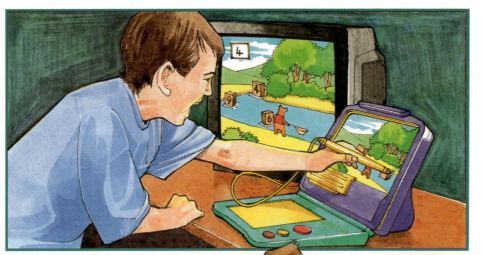

A special pen is connected to a pad plugged into the television. When you use the pen to draw on the pad, the picture appears on the screen. The system can be used in schools.

Interactive television will allow us to take part in a quiz show or choose the course of a football game by pressing buttons on a pad.

Signal receiver

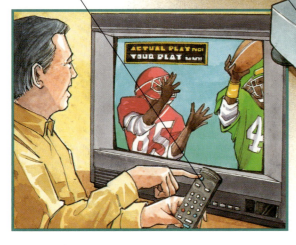

In the future flat screens may be made from light-emitting plastics. These materials give out light when an electric charge is applied to them. The television will have access to libraries and information databanks.

A television screen that rolls up into a pen. The pen holds the receiver electronics.

Flat screen

Speakers

Receiver

In the future
modern electronics will improve radio and television sets. On the radio, music and speech will become much clearer. Television sets will have a larger and clearer picture. The improved system is known as high-definition television. You will be able to talk to your television set, order any film you want, and use your television to play games or go shopping.

USEFUL WORDS

Aerial Part of a radio or television transmitter or receiver which sends or picks up the signals.

Amplifier Device which strengthens electrical signals.

Carrier wave Wave that carries the audio and video signals.

Communications satellite Satellite in space that passes on radio and television signals.

Electromagnetic wave Another name for radio, television and similar waves.

Electron Small particle which carries electricity.

Frequency Number of waves each second.

Loudspeaker Device for changing electrical signals into sound.

Microphone Device for changing sound into electrical signals.

Modulation Process of adding a signal to a carrier wave.

Phosphor Material which glows when hit by electrons.

Receiver Device which picks up radio or television signals and converts them to sound and pictures.

Transmitter Device which makes and sends out radio or television signals.

Tuner Section of a radio or television receiver which picks out the signals from a particular station.

Video tape Tape on which television pictures are recorded.

Wavelength The distance between crests in a wave.